POL
THE KE

and other
nursery rhymes

Illustrated by Carolyn Scrace

CARNIVAL

Polly put the kettle on,
Polly put the kettle on,
Polly put the kettle on,
We'll all have tea.

Sukey take it off again,
Sukey take it off again,
Sukey take it off again,
They've all gone away.

Hey diddle diddle,
The cat and the fiddle,
The cow jumped over the moon;
The little dog laughed
To see such sport,
And the dish ran away with the spoon.

Little Boy Blue,
　　Come blow your horn,
The sheep's in the meadow,
　　The cow's in the corn.

Where is the boy
　　Who looks after the sheep?
He's under a haycock
　　Fast asleep.

Will you wake him?
　　No, not I,
For if I do,
　　He's sure to cry.

Hark, hark,
  The dogs do bark,
The beggars are coming to town;
  Some in rags,
  And some in jags,
And one in a velvet gown.

The Queen of Hearts
She made some tarts,
All on a summer's day;
The Knave of Hearts
He stole those tarts,
And took them clean away.

Ipsey Wipsey spider
  Climbing up the spout;
Down came the rain
  And washed the spider out:
Out came the sunshine
  And dried up all the rain;
Ipsey Wipsey spider
  Climbing up again.

This little pig went to market,
This little pig stayed at home,
This little pig had roast beef,
This little pig had none,
And this little pig cried,
Wee-wee-wee-wee-wee.
All the way home.

Hush-a-bye baby, on the tree top,
When the wind blows, the cradle will rock;
When the bough breaks, the cradle will fall
And down will come baby, cradle and all.

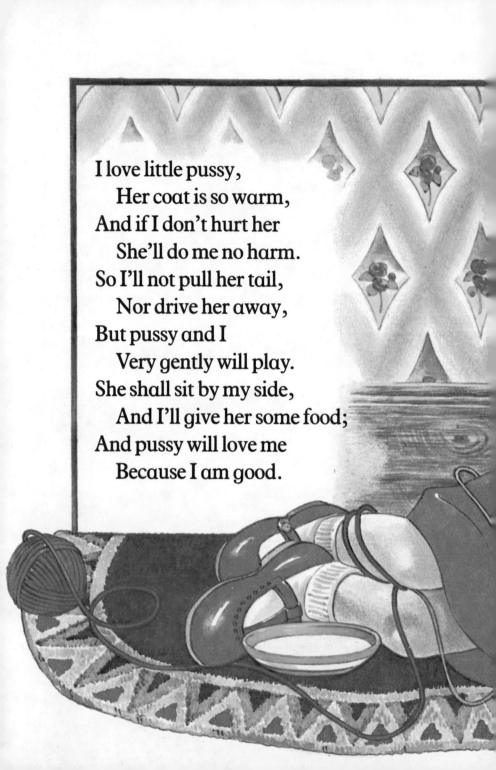

I love little pussy,
    Her coat is so warm,
And if I don't hurt her
    She'll do me no harm.
So I'll not pull her tail,
    Nor drive her away,
But pussy and I
    Very gently will play.
She shall sit by my side,
    And I'll give her some food;
And pussy will love me
    Because I am good.

How many miles to Babylon?
Three-score and ten.
Can I get there by candle-light?
Yes, and back again.
If your heels are nimble and light,
You may get there by candle-light.

A wise old owl sat in an oak,
The more he heard the less he spoke;
The less he spoke the more he heard.
Why aren't we all like that wise old bird?

Oh where, oh where has my little dog gone?
Oh where, oh where can he be?
With his ears cut short and his tail cut long,
Oh where, oh where is he?

Georgie Porgie, pudding and pie,
Kissed the girls and made them cry;
When the boys came out to play,
Georgie Porgie ran away.

Dickery, dickery, dare,
The pig flew up in the air;
The man in brown
Soon brought him down,
Dickery, dickery, dare.

Little Polly Flinders
Sat among the cinders,
Warming her pretty little toes,
Her mother came and caught her,
And whipped her little daughter
For spoiling her nice new clothes.

Pussy cat, pussy cat,
Where have you been?
I've been up to London
To visit the Queen.
Pussy cat, pussy cat,
What did you there?
I frightened a little mouse
Under her chair.

Jack be nimble,
  Jack be quick,
Jack jump over
  The candlestick.